7 THINGS TO DO WHILE WAITING FOR MARRIAGE

(Getting Set For Marriage)

HOPE AMADICHUKWU

CONTENT

INTRODUCTION

Ignorance is a plague and a barrier in life. It is everyman's barrier. It has inhibited many people from going forward in life. Ignorance is not an excuse when it comes to the matter of marriage. It has hindered many marital destinies. When you don't know what to do or how to do it, you will be hindered in life.

Isaiah 5:13. Therefore my people have gone into

captivity, because they have no knowledge; their honourable men are famished and their multitude dried up with thirst.

The only cure for ignorance is acquisition of knowledge. Knowledge is having information about something and when you don't know it, it's called ignorance.

Isaiah 60:2 NKJV for behold, the darkness shall cover the earth, and deep darkness the people; but the Lord will arise over you and His glory will be seen upon you.

This prophecy from the Prophet Isaiah is a reality today. Darkness which implies ignorance is everywhere upon the earth and upon the people. Darkness has not spared the institution of marriage and people including the singles. At the root of many of the reasons for failure in marriage and relationship is ignorance.

That is why in this book, by the inspiration of the Almighty God, I will be unraveling the things to do while waiting for marriage.

We understand from the Bible, that marriage is designed for you to see the goodness of God. If you are not married, God wants you to find goodness. Life before marriage is good, marriage makes it better. ***Gen 2:18 - and the Lord said, 'it is not good that man should be alone; I will make him a helper comparable to him',***

Proverbs 18:22 – He who finds a wife finds a good thing and obtains favour from the Lord.

Ecclesiastes 4:9 – Two are better than one, because they have a good reward for their labour

Singles should not only be filled with the thought of when is the right partner going to come or when they will locate their missing rib. They should also know what to do while waiting for marriage. They should be filled with thoughts of how to discover themselves first, how to impact their world, how to serve God better while still single, they should prepare before marriage. Your level of preparation will determine your performance in marriage.

Marriage is an institution created by God Himself, the first institution that God created and that is why it is worth waiting for. *Genesis 2:18-25.*

Before getting married, there are a lot of things to be done. The bible says in *1Cor.7:32* **but I want you to be without care, he who is unmarried cares for the things of the Lord, how he may please the Lord**. As a single lady/man you stand a better chance of serving God and pleasing him, because there's no distraction as at that time. What to do while waiting for marriage is a book that will make you discover your importance as a single person. Singleness is not a curse but a gift every single should appreciate. Your days of singleness is a blessing you should embrace and not a curse you should detest. There is a greater opportunity to be happy when you are single, because in marriage you must adapt and adopt.

Your years of singleness must not only be the years that you are waiting to marry but the time you are preparing for life and destiny. These are the years you should use to develop yourself.

Having the desire to marry is good but at the same time it's good to be fully prepared for marriage. Most people are not happy because they are single, but I want you to know that being happy as a single is like a seed sown which will eventually reflect in your marriage. Note this, that in marriage you must please your partner and everybody involved in it. Some marriages fail because one partner fails to sacrifice their comfort for the comfort of the other there by leading to disappointment and irreconcilable differences. Some singles rush into marriage and rush out not knowing that it is a journey and they make caricature of it. Some even enter into it for ulterior motives. This is the only institution you get the certificate at the beginning because there's no graduation in marriage, so tread softly and wisely in the path of marriage. Marriage is a covenant not a contract. Marriage means different things to different people. To some it is a necessary evil; to some marriage has been a big pain, to some it is hell on earth. To some it is an organized forum for child bearing and rearing and to some it is a forum for sexual satisfaction and one that will take care of house chores. Please understand that marriage is a life time event and it brings every good thing you so much desire in life. According to Rev. Mrs. Funke Felix Adejumo, Marriage is sweet, depending on the cutlery you use in eating it. If you are a single lady or man looking forward to settle down soon, then this is a must read.

CHAPTER 1

EXPLOIT AND EXPLORE THE BENEFITS OF WAITING

When the purpose of a thing is not known, abuse they say is inevitable. Understanding what it means to wait on God will help you exploit and explore the benefits of waiting. Everyone has got to wait for one thing or the other. Some wait to be promoted, some for-miracle jobs, others wait for a desired miracle. Hannah waited and got the benefits of waiting, Abraham and Sarah waited and they became father and mother of nations.

Hebrews 6:12 – that you do not become sluggish but imitate those who through faith and patience inherit the promises

I want you to understand that between the time of sowing a seed and the time of harvest is called the waiting time, and what you do during the waiting time determines the kind of harvest you will get.

What is the meaning of waiting?

This means to anticipate, to look up to God and to trust him for what he can do.

The waiting time is misunderstood and misused by many, but no man waits for God's purpose and ends in regret. Before God made Eve out of Adam, he made him to understand that while he was waiting for the bone of his bone and the flesh of his flesh, that he could be occupied with work; which was, taking care of the animals and plants. If God says wait, it means he wants to fulfill the requirements of waiting. He says in his word: be still and know that I am God. At the time of writing this book, I had many expectations from God, and the Holy Spirit kept telling me to be still because there's God.

What are the principles of waiting?

1.   Don't faint

Marriage is ordained by God and it's worth waiting for. If you faint in the days of adversity your strength is small. Don't forget that God gives power to the weak and to him who has no might he increases strength. Acknowledging God's sovereign control over all things is one way to show that we are not fainting.

2Corrinthians 4:16 says: For which cause we faint not, but though our outward man perish yet the inward man is renewed day by day.

2. **Trust in God**

    Another principle of waiting is trusting in God and standing on his promises. By doing this, it means you have the full assurance that God can do it. How do you stand on God's promises; by not doubting him, the bible says, God sets the solitary in family. You have to actively

cast your cares on him.
Plugging into God's word
every day to find security
and confidence in him
alone.

*Lamentation 3:25- the
Lord is good unto them
that wait for Him, to the
soul that seeketh Him.*
Don't lose hope while
waiting, though it tarry,
wait. **Habakkuk 2:3.**

Most times we wait on God
for so many things, it is
required we do it with

patience; trust in God for a good marriage and lean not on your own understanding.

3. **You will receive a crown of glory**

The third principle on this write up is knowing that you shall be crowned with God's glory when you wait on him.

1Peter 5:4 when the chief Shepherd appears, you will receive the crown of unfading

glory, which I refer here to a glorious marriage.

4. Know that God will not forsake you.

It's good to have a conviction that God will not forsake you when you wait on him. You may feel completely forgotten by everyone but have it in mind that God cannot forsake you.

Psalm 27:10 when my father and mother forsake me, then the Lord will take me up.

Hebrews 13:5b is a comforting promising scripture that God will never leave those who are his.

Joshua 1:5... so I will be with thee, I will not leave thee nor forsake thee.

God is not a man that he should lie. Your marriage may be delayed does not mean that God has forsaken you, it means God wants to give you a glorious marriage. He may come late because he wants to come big.

5. Be Patient

Waiting can be very hard when you are not patient. Patience is not just waiting but how you wait. It's good to be active in your waiting period. Some render their services to God in their waiting period. If you faint in the days of adversity then your strength is small. Abraham and Sarah waited patiently and became the father and mother of many nations. You need the spirit of patience to be able to wait.

Hebrews 6:12- follow them who through faith and patience inherit the promise.

6.   **Have Faith**

There's need to apply faith in your waiting season. The bible says without faith, it is impossible to please God. To show that you have confidence in God you must wait in faith.

Hebrews 11:1 now faith is the substance of things hoped for and the evidence of things not yet seen.

7. **Don't complain**

Remember what happened to the Israelite when they complained while God was directing them and leading them to their own land, the journey that should have taken few years without struggle took so long and their destiny was delayed. The bible says they that complain will be destroyed by the destroyer. Instead of complaining, rejoice. The same mouth you use in complaining use it to prophecy into your future marriage.

WHAT ARE THE BENEFITS OF WAITING ON GOD FOR A GLORIOUS MARRIAGE?

There are numerous benefits one gets when one waits on God, waiting on Him can never end in futility.

According to *Isaiah 40:31* there are four benefits of waiting. *They that wait on the Lord he shall renew their strength, they shall mount up with wings as eagles, they shall run and not be weary, they shall walk and not faint.*

From this scripture you can see the following benefits:

1. Renewal of strength

2. Mounting up with wings as eagle

3. Running and not being weary

4. Walking and not fainting

1. **The benefits of Renewal
of strength**

Which means God is going
to make an exchange of our
weakness for his strength.
Renewal means God doing a
new thing. He is going to
make all things become new
by bringing you into a new
season, new level, new
heights and everything new.
God is ready to take our
ignorance and give us
supernatural knowledge, he
will bring you into a new

season if you wait. If you don't have the strength of God in you, you can never trust him. You will begin to doubt, that's why you need God's strength to continue trusting him. *Psalm 73:26: My flesh and heart faileth, but God is the strength of my heart and my portion forever. Proverbs 24:10 says if thou faint in the days of adversity, thy strength is small.*

Renewal of strength also means to be strong in your faith, knowing that God is there for you to guide you through. God's strength acts as a shield from feeling of anxiety we may experience. Don't forget that when you fully put your trust in Him, He walks alongside with you.

2. **The benefits of mounting up with wings as eagles.**

Which means while you are waiting, there's supernatural growth and rising, which means to ascend, to climb to a certain height of level in life. Where there will be no more struggles all you need to do is rest on the wind of the Holy Ghost when you soak in his presence.

3. **The benefits of running and not being weary.**

This means waiting and not being tired or giving up.

Waiting on God is like a labour and the bible says for every labour there's a reward. God will not allow you to lose hope, he gives you the supernatural understanding to know that he will not leave you nor forsake you. He will give you the energy and ability to trust on his capacity. It means running to God and him granting you favour and speed to run through.

4. **The benefits of Walking and not fainting:**

This means to proceed, to move, to make progress and things will begin to walk in your favour and in a new dimension in your ways. There will be fresh supply of supernatural strength and faith that will make you wait. There will be speed to scale new heights in all your endeavours.

HOW DO YOU WAIT?

Ask the Holy Spirit to help you. David said in *Psalm 121:1 I will lift up my eyes unto the hills from whence cometh my help and my help comes from the Lord which made heaven and earth.* The Holy Spirit is the third person in the godhead, which is God the Holy Spirit, he is also the custodian of power here on earth and we have to rely on his power in our waiting season. He was here to bring comfort to humanity so if you are fainting in your waiting season, ask Him to help

you.

CHAPTER 2

DISCOVER/DEVELOP YOURSELF

When you discover and develop yourself, you become unique. There is something inside of you that will make you to shine on earth, like a house on a hill that cannot be hidden. Your waiting season is not an idle season, it's a discovery season. The season to discover God's plan and purpose (vision), your potentials and what you are passionate about. By the time you discover and develop yourself you will realize that you can be the best surgeon, the best artist, the best fashion designer, best author and so on and so forth. This will also make you to know your gifts, talents, assignment and calling and once you explore these elements you become fulfilled in life.

Self-discovery and development in your season of waiting for marriage, will make you unique and great. By the time you finally settle in marriage you can be like an institution, a resource, a cistern, a reservoir where people can tap or draw from and of course you cannot be a liability. Marriage is very demanding and you need self-discovery and development to be able to meet the demands of marriage.

Self-discovery gives you a good Knowledge of who you are which gives you the boldness to stand strong. John the Baptist was asked who he was, without hesitating, he gave an answer of who he was and every opposition was silenced. You were created to be at the topmost top, like a city set on a hill that cannot be hidden. You are a trailblazer, Pathfinder and a pace setter. People should be able to follow your footsteps and succeed. Many through you should see light.

1Peter 2:9 we are not common creatures, we were created to be a marvel to our world from darkness to marvelous light.

Amongst others, the following are fundamentals of discovery:

1. Vision (plan and purpose)

2. Potential

3. Passion

4. Talents and skills

What is vision?

A man without a vision is worse than a blind man. He is like a person without direction and future. Vision is the discovery of God's plan and purpose for our lives. Discovering one's purpose on earth is the most exciting thing that can happen to anyone. Everyone created by God was created for a purpose, to impact and affect humanity positively. You were not created to be a liability nor a nonentity but created for a purpose. If you don't know the reason for which you were created you will become a wanderer and a nonentity. *Habakkuk 2:3 for the vision is yet for an appointed time, but at the end it shall speak, and not lie: though it tarry, wait for it: because it will surely come, it will not tarry.* Anyone waiting to get married is supposed to have realized his/her purpose on earth instead of bothering yourself too much about marriage. Am not trying to say that planning to get married is bad but first things first. The time you would have used to get worried is the time to talk to God in prayer to reveal to you the purpose he created you for.

In ***Jeremiah 1:5, he said: before I formed thee, I knew thee, before you were born, I sanctified thee, I ordained you a prophet to all nations. He also said in Jeremiah 33:3 call on me and I will answer you and show you great and mighty things you don't know.***

Anyone that is ignorant of why he or she was created will be confused, unfocused, distracted, misled and limited in life. ***Hosea 4:6 says: my people are destroyed because of lack of knowledge, because you have rejected knowledge, I will reject thee.***

The sky is very big for every star to shine, just discover God's plan and begin to shine. God has a plan for everyone he created, to be creative and innovative.

What is Potential?

The word potential is gotten from the word Omnipotent, meaning that when God made man, he took the potent part of him and poured it into man. Which means that what is in God is exactly what is in us when you give your life to him. ***Matthew 25:15 unto one he gave five talents, to another two, and to another one: to every man according to his several ability....*** Potential is the raw material inside of us, the dormant ability, unused success, hidden treasures, reserved power etc. Potential is what you can be and have not yet become, all you can do and have not yet done. It is something inside of a man that needs to be discovered and used to the glory of God. It is a hidden success. You can go far in life once you maximize it. Every child of God is endowed with potential to make you shine on earth.

HOW TO DEVELOP YOUR POTENTIAL

❖ Define your goals

- ❖ Explore what you have values for and care about
- ❖ Develop new skills
- ❖ Be open minded and learn something new

WHAT IS PASSION?

Passion is a strong feeling of love for something. Passion is an emotion to be acted upon. Without action, passion yields no worthwhile results. It is the fuel in the fire of action. When you have passion for something, you love doing it, even when you are not paid for it. Passion can push you through difficult times because you don't care what it takes to become better.

HOW TO KNOW WHAT YOU ARE PASSIONATE ABOUT?

Passion drives you, gives you limitless energy to go for what you are passionate about, it motivates and pushes you. You will never know what you are truly capable of doing unless you push yourself to do it. One can be passionate about anything good in life. Passion most times can lead us to fulfilling God's plan and purpose in life. If you have undying love to effect a change in a particular area, it could be your passion. For instance, I have the passion to make people know the truth about living right and having a good knowledge about marriage, relationship or other important areas, so it pushes me to write a book, or to communicate God's faithfulness to the world and I do that by singing or public speaking. Passion is something you do even if you will not be paid for it, even if it will cost you millions to get it done, you really don't mind. Do you have the passion to see souls saved? It could be a pointer to you being a doctor or a pastor, or do you have undying love to communicate the gospel to the world? Which can be done through singing, acting or dancing. Think of what you have undying love for, it could be a pointer to your fulfilling destiny.

WHAT PASSION WILL DO

1. It will increase self confidence

2. It will boost self esteem

3. It will/might make you smarter

4. It will make you more resilient

5. It can boost your performances

TALENT AND SKILLS

Talent refers to an inborn and the special ability of a person to do something. A skill is an expertise, which is acquired by the person by learning. Talent is God gifted ability, whereas skill is an ability in which you put your time and efforts to develop. Talents could be expressed through the following: writing (books and song), singing, sports, acting, dancing, public speaking, teaching, humor etc.

Example of Skills could be: computer, problem solving, communication, leadership, management, time management, handwork skills etc.

Your vision, potentials, passions, talent and skill can lead to the full discovery of yourself, explore these areas and you will be fulfilled in life.

How do you develop your vision?

Self-discovery is not life fulfilled. By the time you discover you vision, you know your potentials and purpose you have to work with them to achieve your goals in life. Discovery is not fulfillment; your discovery alone does not bless any one until you work it out or you run with it.

Communicate your vision to others – you can develop your vision by communicating it others. No one can decide to follow you until they know what direction you are heading. Every vision must bring solution to mankind and move people towards achieving common goal, which is why your vision must be communicated to others. Your vision should inspire others to discover their own. When people are inspired they are more likely to work on something that will better their lives.

Find role models you can look up to – looking up to others who have attained certain height in marriage and life can inspire and motivate you for self-development.

Find a mentor - this can be anyone who knows something you don't know and you are ready to learn from the person. This is somebody that is more experienced who is willing to take you under their wings.

CHAPTER 3

INVEST

What is Investment? According to Ecclesiastes 11:1 investment is casting your bread upon many waters, which you will find profit in abundance after many days. It can be likened to a seed in your hands, that, if it is not planted it will yield no fruit, no harvest. *Warren Buffet defined investment as forgoing consumption now in order to have the ability to consume more at a later date.*

Where do you invest?

1. Invest in yourself

2. Do a business investment

3. Create multiple streams of income

What does the bible say about investment?

The bible teaches that it's needful to wisely save and invest for the future. *Ecclesiastes 11:1 says, cast your bread upon the waters, for you will find it after many days.*

1. **INVEST IN YOURSELF**

How do you invest in yourself?

- **Learn new skills** – learning never ends. A great way to invest in yourself is to keep learning. This may actually be dependent on your current endeavours, look out for new skills that will help you succeed in your current job or career for instance, you can learn time management, playing of musical instrument e.t.c. which will help you create a better life and lead to greater overall satisfaction. You can also learn new skills on your own by reading books.

- **Read and Study** – this can also help you build skills that can improve your career prospects. Reading is good for the brain because it can take you into critical thinking, skills promote quicker thinking and help prevent cognitive decline. You have to read a lot of books on marriage in your waiting season to equip you with the right knowledge on investment in marriage proper. This may cost you some money, but it's rather you pay the price now to get the prize later. The prize of information is better than the price of illiteracy. Formal education is good, often times the degrees are structured in only one way. But informal like audio books, eBooks or seminars attended where certain area is focused on can help you to a great extent.

- **Find a mentor** – this is someone who can stretch you, who can take you to where you have never been and where you are supposed to be, who knows what you don't know. Growth most times happens in the exposure to new concepts. You can't stay in the same place and understand everything, you need someone who knows it more than you do, who would take your hand and show you the way. When you don't have exposure, you make quick commitment because you don't have all the information.

- **Network with people that will help your net-worth –** the closest people to you will influence and affect where you will reach in life. If everybody around you is lesser than you and they are not challenging you, it means you don't have empires, in other ways; you have not invested in yourself.

- **Attend seminars and workshops** – these are excellent opportunities for investing in yourself for good reasons. These events help to expand your knowledge in an area or field you are already familiar with, like in the field of marriage, there are seminars and workshops on marriage that every single can attend.

2. DO A BUSINESS INVESTMENT

These are tools that can help you achieve your financial goals. One can invest in bank products like savings or invest in buying of shares with different companies. When you buy shares, you are buying an ownership stake in that company. Simply put, a share is a percentage of ownership in a company. Investors who hold shares of any company are known as shareholders. Some companies like: MTN, UP Plc, etc invest by raising funds from investors. They also allow stakeholders a stake in the company's profits. Before going into any investment, seek a professional's advice.

How much should you use for investment?

You must not wait until you have a lot of money before you start an investment. This is dependent on your financial situation and your investment goals. You could even start investing in stock with as low as =N=50,000.00. So, the amount to invest with is up to you.

There are other types of investment like bonds, bank products, retirement savings, savings for education, annuities etc. please go for adequate knowledge on this before going into it. Though there are risks involved, but don't forget it is risky not to take a risk. Explore these areas and make money while waiting.

3. CREATE MULTIPLE STREAMS OF INCOME

With this changing economy one may not need to rely on only one source of income to survive. To be financially stable, you need multiple streams of income. Having this means earning money from different avenues. Without another income stream, your business might fail. Many people have a single income stream such as being an electrician; teacher etc. having multiple streams is a good way of safeguarding your business against a downturn. It can give your business stability and opportunity to grow.

There are two types of income streams: active and passive.

Active income stream is where you do some work or provide a service and someone pays you for it.

Passive income is where the income is not directly tied to the work you do. Although, it is called passive income, there is still work required to do to generate the revenue. It doesn't come for free. The work needed for a passive income stream takes place earlier on, and the income comes later and for a lifetime. An example of this is to build an online store. The work at the beginning is to build the website, upload your products and promote them. The passive income comes later as people begin to buy products from your store. It is called passive because people can buy products when you are asleep. They say "Don't put all your eggs in one basket" which means don't concentrate on one thing and it also applies particularly to spreading your income stream in excellent way of earning more money and reducing risk.

There are seven ways to generate income, which are as follows:

Earned income, profit income, interest income, dividend income, rental income, capital gains income and royalty income.

Earned Income – this is a primary income stream through a job. This is very limiting and has the acronym (JOB) Just Over Broke. This means to earn just enough to survive. Some jobs pay exceptionally well, but these are exceptions not the norm.

Profit Income – by rendering a service or selling a product for what they cost. This is being self-employed or an entrepreneur. It takes to achieve the goals here and there are risks but at the long run, the gains will be more.

Interest Income – this is buying government bonds that will generate interest.

Dividend Income – the gains made from buying of shares. It can generate excellent passive income streams.

Rental Income – the money generated from the properties you rent. This is also a passive income.

Capital Income – buying and selling of assets. For example, if you buy stocks or shares for N50,000.00 and sell them for N70,000.00 the capital gain is N20,000.00.

Royalty Income – this is generated by designing, building or making something unique and charging people for making use of it. Musicians are a prime example of this. Some musicians are signed to a particular label of a recording company. The recording company produces the records, market and sell them. The musician receives a royalty payment for every album sold and every time it is played to the public.

Types of passive income

Writing an eBook, rental income, creating a blog or YouTube channel, selling of products online, etc.

Types of active income

Active refers to income received for performing a service. Like wages, salaries, commissions e.t.c. from any employment. Active income is generated from tasks linked to your job or career that takes up time. For example, you are paid a certain amount of money called salary, for the company you provide services to. If you are working for a person or a company, be it manual labour, office work or home-based service, you earn active income.

Passive income is income you can earn with relatively minimal effort, such as renting out a property or earning money from a business without much active participation.

CHAPTER 4

BEWARE OF JOY STEALERS

Joy according to the bible is a feeling of good pleasure and happiness that is dependent on who Jesus is rather than who we are or what is happening around us. Joy comes from the Holy Spirit, abiding in God's presence and from hope in his word. ***John 16:22...and your joy no man taketh from you. Philippians 4:4 "Rejoice in the Lord always, and again I say, rejoice."*** Joy is a fruit of the spirit. Joy and laughter are weapons of the spirit, the bible says he that sits on throne shall laugh. Joy is not the same thing as momentary happiness; it is part of the fruit of the spirit.

What are the dimensions of joy?

The joy of salvation – this is the dimension of joy that comes when we receive Jesus. This is the salvation through faith in Jesus Christ. It's an experience that brings deliverance, restoration and preservation. It is deliverance from the grip of satan, a restoration from eternal shame. It is not controlled by physical circumstances of life. Even in the midst of trials and tribulations of life, you can still have this joy. It is evidence of salvation. If you are born again, then you must have this joy. (*1Peter 1:8...though now you do not see him, yet believing, you rejoice with joy inexpressible and full of glory*).

The joy of walking in purpose —
there is a fulfillment you get when you walk in purpose, it gives you joy.

Purpose fulfilled, produces joy. Once you have found your place in life and destiny, transforming lives, producing results by engaging the word consistently it brings joy unspeakable.

What did Paul say about us losing our joy?

According to *Philippians 4:4 rejoice in the Lord always and again I say rejoice*. Joy comes from a melody that mocks your situations. *Nehemiah 8:10 - the*

joy of the Lord is our strength. It means when you lack joy, you lack strength. The solution to any challenge may not be readily available but joy is always available if you want it, because it is a fruit of the spirit of God. Your waiting season needs joy to keep you through, even if there is no husband or wife your joy must be intact. Count it all joy. Do not allow anything steal your joy, don't cheat yourself by being gloomy, rejoice because joy brings harvest. They that sow in tears shall reap in joy.

In the midst of pain, stay in joy, once you lose your joy, you are about losing everything. Once you focus on the pain, it will start growing and you may not have the victory again. The marriage breakthrough you need is in your joy. Being joyful after prayer is a sign that God has answered your prayers. The bible says ask that your joy may be full. Weeping endures for a night, but joy must come in the morning. Where righteousness, peace and joy coexist, there's the kingdom of God. You can turn any situation around if you understand the mystery of joy. Extreme and exceeding joy is unexplainable. Satan has lost it over your tears, he has no opportunity to see your tears again. They looked unto him and were not afraid because of joy. Have the fullness of joy. How can your joy be full? The bible says ask that your joy may be full.

What is the condition to have strength?

The bible says only with joy shall we draw water out of the wells of salvation. You need your joy to be intact in your waiting season, because the joy of the Lord is always our strength. Once you lose your joy, you lose your strength, that's why you must beware of joy stealers. It is very mandatory to maintain a joyful mood when you are single because it will reflect eventually in your marriage.

What does the book of Philippians say about joy?

The book of Philippians teaches us how to experience the joy of the Lord that is ours in Christ. It is often known as the epistle of joy because Paul was writing to the saints at Philippi while he was in prison, telling them to rejoice. He had every reason to be discontent and upset instead rejoicing in every circumstance and finding joy amidst trials. His top priority was to show joy and preach on humanity. It's a mystery that while Paul had every earthly reason to be angry, proud, complain or question God's plan, he not only chose to rejoice but also encouraged the Philippians to always rejoice. Instead of being filled with fear and anxiety he chose ultimate contentment and prayer. I believe that Paul's situation is an example of the worst condition one could find himself. The prison is not a conducive atmosphere for one to be in the right frame of mind not to even talk of putting others in the same state. Your condition may not be or may be worse than Paul's own but I encourage you to rejoice evermore because the Lord is about to do what no man can do, he's about to give you a glorious marriage he's about to turn your mourning into dancing, congratulations.

What does it mean to have a fullness of joy?

In the fullness of joy, there is no sorrow, worry, doubt or fear in the fullness of joy, there's abundant life, peace, freedom and love. ***Psalm 43:4 then I will go unto the altar of God, to God my exceeding*** *joy, and on the harp, I will*

praise you, o God.

JOY STEALERS

There are attitudes, behaviors, and actions that will stop you from being able to experience the joy of the Lord in your life. Don't let anyone steal your joy else it will make your life to look miserable. The spirit of Joy is so important in our lives, and we should guard it with all our heart and not let anyone or anything steal it from us. No situation or circumstance has the right to detect how we should feel per time. Whatever steals your joy has taken your power. That is why it's so important to protect our joy and not let anyone take it away from us.

Below are the joy stealers you must be aware of in your waiting season. This will help you maintain focus. So, remain joyful while you're waiting.

1. **Jealousy** – this can easily steal your joy as a single, seeing that you are not yet settled and perhaps everyone around you is

getting engaged on daily basis, the emotion of jealousy sets in. When you look at someone else and imagine how great their life is while grumbling about what you lack is what is known as jealousy. It should be completely avoided because it can steal your joy and one can overcome jealousy by being focused on the goals of life you have already set and also ensuring that you work hard relentlessly to achieve them.

2. **Fear** - The fear of inadequacy or not being good enough can ruin your life. Most times it's called the fear of the unknown. What are you afraid of? The fear that age is no longer on your side may come in if you are not guided, there's good news the bible speaking in *Isiah 41:10 fear not for I am with you, be not dismayed, for I am your God. I will strengthen you, yes, I will help you, I will uphold you with my righteous right*

hand. Do not feel insecure, intimidated or timid because you are single, don't forget singleness is a blessing.

3. **Comparison/Envy -** this is having your eyes on another person's achievement. If you do this you will easily get discouraged in your waiting season *"Comparison is the enemy of joy."* According to *Mark Twain*. It is aimless to compare one's self to another person because everyone was

created differently and with different destiny. The road to your destination will definitely not be the same with mine. Comparison makes you feel limited. It limits one's thought and mindset. Everyone has its own uniqueness in life and according *to Ecclesiastes 3:1 there is time for everything under the sun.* Your time of rising may not be another person's own and that does not mean you are less human because definitely you are also going to have your own time of rising. We are all on our own unique journey in life, and comparing ourselves to others will only hold us back from achieving our goals. So, avoid it!

Envy is ugly. It makes us hate people for being blessed. Don't be envious of someone, especially when you don't know what challenges they're faced with. One way to avoid envy is to understand that not everyone is called to do the same thing. Even more, no one person is called to do everything. Romans *12:6-8* *makes this clear: "Having gifts that differ according to the grace given to us, let us use them: if prophecy, in proportion to our faith; if service, in our serving; the one who teaches, in his teaching; the one who exhorts, in his exhortation; the one who contributes, in generosity; the one who leads, with zeal; the one who does the act of mercy, with cheerfulness".* (Romans 12:6-8 ESV)

To stop comparison and envy from stealing our joy, we must seek God, not others for our gifts and purposes. God gives each person unique gifts specific to what He has purposed for them to accomplish. The only way to know what those gifts are and to fulfill the purpose He has given us is to seek Him, not how someone else is doing it. When we become clear on this, we have no reason to be jealous or envious and make more room for joy in our lives.

4. **Complain** – a complainer is one who has lost his/her joy. Paul told the Philippians not to complain but to maintain their joy. ***"Do all things without grumbling or disputing,***

that you may be blameless and innocent, children of God without blemish in the midst of a crooked and twisted generation, among whom you shine as lights in the world." (Philippians 2:14-15 ESV)

You cannot complain and be grateful at the same time. Once you have lost your joy, you become ungrateful. When you complain, you look no different from the world. Instead of complaining it is better to be thankful so as to maintain your joy and get your harvest. The bible says they that complain shall be destroyed by the destroyer.

5. **Pride** - Paul remained joyful through humility *(Phil 2:4-8-* ***Look not every man on his own things, but every man also on the things of others).*** When we think we deserve better, we become bitter and pride must set in.

pride as a joy stealer puts you under an emotion that makes you feel God is supposed to have given you a kind of life style instead of the one you are living. Being humble is acknowledging God's faithfulness in our lives at every point in time. Nevertheless, there is room to ask for more according to the bible in **Matthew 7:7** instead of allowing our joy to leave us. *(Phil 2:12) Wherefore, my beloved, as ye have always* *obeyed, not as in my presence only, but now much more in my absence, work out your own salvation with fear and trembling.* We need to walk with "fear and trembling."

6. **Sin** - Sinful living brings about sorrow and death. *(Phil 3:19) Whose end is destruction, whose God is their belly, and whose glory is in their shame, who mind earthly*

things. When we are controlled by our fleshly desires, we will lose our joy. Holiness is happiness.

7. Anxiety - this steals space in our hearts and mind where God's peace should be. In turn, it always takes our joy. Instead of being anxious we should be prayerful. Instead of worrying, we should be thankful and expectant *(Proverbs 23:18 – for surely there is an end and your expectation shall*

not be cut off). This is how we overcome anxiety to live the joyful life that is ours in Christ. *Philippians 4:6 be anxious for nothing, but by prayer and supplication with thanksgiving, make your requests known unto God*

8. **Bitterness** – It steals our joy and personal relationship with God. Bitterness is the anger we have held unto until it has gained the power. Bitterness is

a stealer and will not allow one to fulfill destiny. John the Baptist was a core victim of bitterness and he paid with his life by being bitter with Jesus.

Ephesians 4:31 let all bitterness and wrath and anger and clamor and slander be put away from you, along with all malice.

Proverbs 14:10 the heart knows its own bitterness, and a stranger does not share its joy.

9. **Depression** – this another enemy that comes to steal our joy, kill our peace, destroy our identity. The goal of the enemy is to diminish that which makes us attractive to others and that which might attract them to God. When you are joyful, you attract good people to yourself. John *15:11 **I have told you this so that my joy may be in you and that your joy may be complete.***

CHAPTER 5

STAY IN THE RIGHT RELATIONSHIP

What is a relationship?

A relationship is any connection between two people, which can be either positive or negative. To be in a relationship does not always mean there is physical intimacy, emotional attachment and or commitment involved, people engage in different types of relationship that have unique characteristics.

<u>Types of Relationships</u>

- ❖ **Family relationship** – this is relatedness or connection by blood or marriage or adoption. It can also be a group of two or more persons related by birth, marriage or adoption who live together. All such related persons are considered as members of one family.

- ❖ **Friendship** - this is a relationship of mutual affection between people. It is a stronger form of interpersonal bond than an acquaintance or association, such as classmate, neighbor or colleague. Friends can help you celebrate good times and provide support during bad times. They can also increase your sense of belonging and purpose, enrich your life and improve your health.

* **Acquaintances** – this is a state of being familiar with someone, a person known to one, but usually not a close friend.

* **Romantic and Sexual relationship** – this is having feelings of attraction for another person which involves obsession, intimacy and commitment. It can also be defined as a relationship

involving sexual intimacy, which should be for the married.

HOW DO YOU KNOW A RELATIONSHIP IS RIGHT?

A relationship is right when the following are observed:

1. When God is the ultimate – putting God first

2. When the relationship is defined

3. When boundaries are set

4. When love is defined according to 1Corrinthians 13:4-8

5. When there is self-control

1. A relationship is right when God is the ultimate.

A good relationship will put God first before self and pleasure, rather God as their priority. Any relationship that takes you away from the presence of God is not a good relationship. If you are trying to live a life that honours God, then you must be in a relationship that honours God as a single. Please this should not be compromised. To ensure that God is an important factor in your life, then choose someone who is godly. A godly relationship will put God first and the basis of every of their actions is on the word of God. If you put him first, it will strengthen the relationship. If you want God to be the central in your relationship, then choose someone who is passionate about God. Get involved with a partner that displays godly qualities like: patience, kindness, humility, self-control etc. it will be very difficult to make God the centre of your relationship when you are in a relationship with an unbeliever. A godly relationship is God focused. He should be the priority over you. Which means there is a point you should not go beyond in the activities of the relationship.

2. A relationship is right when the relationship is defined

Most times, people go into a relationship with wrong motives and deceit, at times to have a fling, to satisfy sexual urge or because of peer influence. A relationship that is defined should be the one that should have great visions or possibly lead to marriage destination. You should only be in a relationship when the other party is a potential life-long partner. Most relationship are not defined and this give room for intimacy when it is not supposed to be so and should be avoided until you are married. Before going into a relationship, ask yourself why and ask the other person what for? Else you will end up in regret. A person of purpose would not want to be distracted with a casual dating, which is very popular in the circular world.

A relationship that is defined should be able to answer the following questions:

> Why the relationship?

> Where is it leading to, marriage or just casual dating?

> What would be the activities of the relationship?

> What is the vision of the relationship?

> Is it a relationship to satisfy sexual urge?

> Is it going to help me fulfill purpose in life?

> Is it going to bring good tidings?

> Does my partner see me as a spouse or sex partner?

Once these questions are properly answered, then both parties are doing the right thing.

3. A relationship is right when boundaries are set.

What are boundaries?

Boundaries are limits that are placed in a relationship that one must not go beyond. When your boundaries are observed by the other party, it means they have respect and value for you and for themselves. Boundaries are set in a relationship to make you focus.

What boundary do you set?

Sexual boundaries. Once this is done, it will make both parties to know the lines they should not cross. Sexual boundaries like no kissing, no hugging, no touching, no holding of hands; why, because all of these leads to sex and after sex definitely, unwanted pregnancy must set in which will later make the lady to take up abortion as the last option. Keeping sexual urge in check will help you not to be intimate before marriage. Please, do not compromise, sex after marriage is worth waiting for.

4. A relationship is right when love is defined according to 1Corrinthians 13:4-8

Love is not lust and love is not infatuation. Most times, these two are mistaken for love. Before defining love according to the scripture, let us look at the true meaning of love. The scripture above should be the basis for which our love is expressed. Love is displeasing yourself to show care without any benefit. For God so loved the world that he gave his only begotten son, who so believe in him will not perish but have everlasting life. This is the agape love God showered on us while we were yet sinners, he died for us. If there's no sacrifice there is no love

According to 1Corinthians 13:4-8

Love is displeasing ourselves to please God or another. When we commit sexual immorality, we are displeasing God to please our flesh, because God is not pleased when we commit sin. The bible says that marriage is bed undefiled and whoremongers God shall judge. The scripture says love is patient, kind, it does not envy, does not boast, it is not proud, it does not dishonour others, it is not self-seeking, it is not easily angered, it keeps no record of wrong, does not delight with evil but rejoices with the truth. It always protects, always trusts, always hopes and always perseveres. Love never fails. Any other definition that goes contrary to this is a wrong definition of love. If your partner is forcing you to have sex with him or her, to prove that you love them, please it is not love it is lust and a show of lack of self-control and also another way to displease God. Love does not think evil, does not rejoice in iniquity but in truth. (having sex before marriage is rejoicing in iniquity) When you define love in your relationship according to the attributes of 1Corrianthians 13:4-8 I will agree with you that you are in the right relationship.

5. A relationship is right when there is self-control

There's need to have self-control over everything in life including the desire to have sex. Paul said in *1Corrinthians 9:27 I bring my body under subjection*. One of the qualities a Christian should exhibit is called temperance which means self-control, having control over desires, bringing them under subjection, because by the time you allow the desires to have control over you, you might be led by the devil and strange gods to commit sin. Sex is not bad, but having sex before marriage is disobedience to God's word. That is why God said in Deuteronomy 28:1 if thou will hearken diligently. In a godly relationship there is self-control. When a man/woman is telling you that the relationship must involve sex, then he/she is telling you that he/she does not have self-control. When you are in a relationship that there is no self-control it means in marriage there will be no self-control because whatever you sow in a relationship is what you will get in marriage. Allow your relationship to glorify God, let people know it is possible to abstain from sex till you are legally married.

What are the things to avoid in a relationship?

Avoid Intimacy (Sex)

Abstinence from sex before marriage is possible. God himself created sex for a purpose, but it is a pity that the reason it was being created for is greatly misunderstood by many today. The bible says marriage should be bed undefiled and whoremongers shall be judged. Hebrews 13:4 meaning sex before marriage should not be encouraged. Sex is worth waiting for and some of the reasons God created sex for was for intimacy and procreation. In Genesis 1:28 he told them to be fruitful and multiply and replenish the earth, what he actually meant was go and have sex and have children. The desire to have sex was put into man by God himself. It is not wrong to have such feelings, but everyone should wait for the right time for such feelings to be expressed. Sex must be done in the context of marriage.

The problem is not because God put the desire in man but the problem is that most singles are not patient enough to wait and don't know how to control the desire before marriage.

Most singles have sex before marriage because they want to enjoy the pleasure of sex and there is this belief that everybody is doing it and it is not possible to wait till marriage before sex. There is no need to rush for sex because throughout your life time in marriage you will enjoy it. There is always much to gain in abstaining from sexual immorality and there is always much to lose when you indulge in sexual intimacy before marriage. The grace to abstain from pre-marital sex is available, take advantage of this grace and you see yourself staying out of it. You can overcome the urge by putting your focus on achieving your endeavours in life, avoid pornography and people that will encourage it in your life. Books and places that portray this should be avoided.

Avoid Long courtship. If a courtship has lasted for more than two years, then both parties should be very watchful and be careful. A long relationship is dangerous except it has a good vision. When there is constant meeting with the opposite sex, there's bound to be a lot of temptations and the urge to have sex will be there. A relationship that is defined may not necessarily stay for too long before marriage except both parties have agreed to stay for a long time for a good reason and are willing to abstain from anything that will spoil the relationship.

The question now is, when should one go into a relationship?

When the man is prepared and must be ready to leave and

cleave and the woman is ready to be a wife:

The bible says a man shall leave his father and mother and shall cleave to his wife and they two shall be one flesh. Which means there must be a leaving before a cleaving. If you are not ready to take up the responsibility of leaving and cleaving as a man then you should not start any good relationship. Are you ready to take up the responsibility of being a husband/father/priest, a wife/mother/minister? Marriage is not for boys, but for men according to the bible. Being a man or wife is not by age but by the readiness of the mind to take up responsibilities. ***Proverbs 19:14b says a prudent wife is from the Lord. Proverbs 18:22 says whoso finds a wife, finds a good thing***. When you are ready to be a wife, you can go into a relationship with the opposite sex. When a man is ready to leave his father and mother then he can cleave, when he is ready to be independent then he can go into a godly relationship. when he/she knows, understands and have the ability to tolerate to have self-control.

My experience

I personally have a testimony when I and my husband were in courtship. When he approached me, I saw a young man who was ready with great visions and full of purpose. We received the grace to abstain from sex. Visiting him at home, washing and cooking for him was highly prohibited. During our courtship, a lot of things were established, which are the pillars and foundation our marriage is standing on. After six months of courtship we got married.

How were we able to achieve this?

By setting boundaries, defining the relationship, making sure we met in an environment that was not conducive for sexual intercourse. Instead, we resorted to making use of environments like the church or eateries and our anchor scripture was Hebrews 13:4.

Where there no temptations?

Yes, there were, but I saw that six months of abstinence from sex will give me life time peace and joy and a stable marriage, which is what I am enjoying in marriage till tomorrow.

What did we avoid?

We avoided situations that would make us to be tempted. So instead of touching we were talking.

If you want God to be the center of your relationship, it is good to avoid people, places and situations where you might be tempted to do the things you know will displease God. Situations like partying, clubbing, watching movies on TV shows that contain graphic sex or violence should be avoided instead occasions like picnic, sports, or wholesome media that will enrich or educate you can be encouraged.

CHAPTER 6

BE A KINGDOM STEWARD

Stewardship is about managing God's resources. While waiting for marriage, kingdom endeavour must be your priority. Who is a kingdom steward? Every believer serving God and the interest of his kingdom. When you serve God, you become blessed beyond measures. ***Exodus 23:25 And you shall serve the Lord your God and he shall bless your bread and your water***. The time you are waiting is the best time to serve God. When you sow a seed of serving God genuinely, your generations unborn will also reap the harvest. Knowing God is the greatest thing that can happen to any man on earth. If you are a sinner and you don't know God, you are still dwelling in the past, having the old nature and losing a lot. The bible says in ***2Corrinthians 5:17 if any man be in Christ, he is a new creature, old things are passed away and all things are become new.*** The power of God is released on us when we accept Christ as our Lord and saviour. ***John 1:12 says for as many as received him, to them he gave the power to become the sons of God.*** If you don't know God, the power to abstain from sin will not be there. The bible says we should serve God in our youthful age, be dedicated and diligent in service to God. Serving God in spirit and in truth keeps your mind off sin, having fellowship with Christ is living a Christ-like life, which is a life to please God, a life of obedience, a life of consecration and would love to say that godliness is profitable unto all things 1Timothy 4:18, including abstaining from premarital sex. Fellowship time is word time and once this time is used for something else, like engaging in sin, you stand to lose a lot. *Hebrew 10:25 says not forsaking the assembling of ourselves together, as is the manner of some but exhorting one another and so much the more as you see the day approaching.*

How to serve God as a single?

Remember why you were called

- we are called primarily to serve God and by doing this we get our blessings. Singles do play major roles in the kingdom of God, because they serve without being distracted. *1Corrinthians 7:22 says: he that is unmarried cares for the things that belongs to the Lord, how he may please the Lord.*

David as the case study

There is something David was doing when God found him. He was serving.

"I have found David my servant. I will make him stand and the enemy will not be able to resist him". Where do you want God to find you? Is it in the place of service or the other way round? If you don't serve, you may not be found by God. While serving God, you can locate your life partner because Jesus said, *"him will his father honour that serve me"*. David had a heart for God, he was passionate concerning the things of God, his zeal was noticed. Service is the place of discovery, a place of learning. You cannot be a good leader

until you are a good servant. ***Joshua 24:15c as for me and my house, we will serve the Lord. John 2:17b the zeal of thine house hath eaten me up, Psalm 69:9a for the zeal of thine house hath eaten me up.***

Advantage of being a single

Singles have more freedom to devote themselves fully to God and his service. Paul points out that the single person has more time to devote to serving God than a married person does. Marriage has certain responsibilities that takes time and effort which otherwise could have been given to God. This notwithstanding both married and single people can be fully devoted to the Lord. But his emphasis is that the single person can do more, since he does not have the family obligations that a married person has.

Marriage is an honourable and holy relationship when we follow God's law. Our purpose in life is not only to get married or remain single, but to glorify God. ***Ecclesiastes 12:13 let us hear the conclusion of the whole matter: fear God and keep his commandments for this is the whole duty of man.*** Being single does not make you more or less valueable to God. God has given all Christians; married or single, a part in the body of Christ. 1Corrinthians 12:14 – 26.

People who served God faithfully while single

Apostle Paul was single and served God faithfully till the end

1. Prophet Ezekiel was a widower, he also did

2. John the baptizer was single, he also did

3. Jesus was single and today the whole universe is celebrating him because of his service unto God.

A single person can faithfully serve God. ***Colossians 3:24 – knowing that of the Lord ye shall receive the reward of the inheritance for ye serve the Lord Christ.*** If you are single, you have more time to serve God. Apostle Paul viewed singleness as a gift. *1Corrinthians 7:7 for I would that all men were even as I myself. But every man hath his proper gift of God, one after this manner and another after that.*

Marriage is good and honourable before God so is being single. If you are single, you are just as important to God and to the body of Christ. Abel had no family, Boaz married quite late in life, *Ruth 4:13 so Boaz took*

Ruth and she was his wife, and when he went in unto her, the Lord gave her conception and she bore a son. Anna, the prophetess lived 84years unmarried and served God faithfully. *Luke 2:37 and she was a widow of about fourscore and four years, which departed not from the temple, but served God with fastings and prayers night and day.*

<u>**How can singles serve God more effectively while waiting?**</u>

❖ **Serve Faithfully** - While waiting for God to provide you with a lifetime partner serve God faithfully, God is a rewarder of them who diligently seek him, while seeking him, you are serving him and he will reward you. *Proverb 19:14 states that a prudent wife is from the lord*. That also applies to a prudent husband as well.

❖ **Serve Tirelessly** – Galatians 6:9 says do not be weary in well doing. Service is not a burden; it is pleasurable. Don't get tired of serving God, don't relent, and don't give up.

* **Serve with a Reward Mindset** – have the mindset that your service to God will not be in vain. We receive priceless blessings when we serve God.

* **Serve with Zeal and Passion** – be zealous and passionate about your service

to God. Don't be casual in your service to God. See it as a treasure and let your heart be there. The bible says where ever a man's treasure is there will his heart be. So be focused and serious about service. Take your service like if you are not there no other person will be available to do it.

❖ **Take service as a business**
– when service is taken as a business you ensure that you

make profit from it, which is the essence of doing business. How do you treat a business? Serve God the same way, Jesus said "him will my father honour". One of the profits for service is honour, which cannot be gotten outside service. There's heavenly pay for every one that serves God, which no man can afford to pay you.

TO BE AN EFFECTIVE CHRISTIAN AS A SINGLE TWO AREAS WILL BE EXAMINED

1. Know that we were called to serve God. We are all primarily called to do the work of God which he has set before us to grow and develop ourselves spiritually. We have a unique calling to prepare for rulership as a king and a priest. Revelation 5:10. As a single or married know that we are called

to build tomorrow as the bride
of Christ.

2. Singles play major roles in
God's church, because
*1Corrinthians 1:32 says he
that is unmarried cares
for the things that belong
to him, how he may serve
and please the Lord.* Ensure
you are involved in fellowship
actively to attract the blessings
of God. *Galatians 6:9 let us
not be weary in well doing,*

we shall reap if we faint not. The time you are single is the right time to build the foundation and put God first. Matthew 6:33

3. Value your spiritual family – Matthew 19:29. Look forward to serving your fellow Christian at every opportunity. Serve the family in your capacity as a single. Maintain a high standard spiritually, morally, in conversation, in dressing, in

manner and be always conscious that you are a king and a priest.

Benefits of serving God

1. Allows us to experience miracles John 2:1

2. Allows us to experience joy and peace that comes from obedience of service

3. Service increases our faith

4. Allows us to experience God's presence

The following are the best ways to serve God as a single

1. Serve God with your financial resources

- Through tithing Malachi 3:10

- Through giving towards the promotion of the kingdom

2. Serve God by winning souls

3. Use your talent/creativity to serve God

4. By praying for the kingdom - Matthew 6:9-10. This is prayer for the promotion of God's kingdom, for souls to be saved

and be established in the kingdom

While you are waiting, one of the best things to do is to serve God and you won't regret it, the reward will be overwhelming and everyone will see the blessings of God upon your life.

CHAPTER 7

PRAY FOR YOUR FUTURE MARRIAGE

The place of prayer can never be over emphasized when it comes to marriage. You don't only pray for marriage when you are in marriage but before and after marriage. *Jeremiah. 33:3 says call on me and I will show you great and mighty things you don't know.* Spending your life time with someone who is different from you is not quite easy but the grace is sufficient and that's why you need to pray. Marriage has its ups and downs, there's disagreement then agreement, there's breaking and then making. Praying for your marriage is one of the most rewarding things you can do for your marriage relationship. If you make prayer your priority and not an option then handling a lot of issues will be much easier.

What is prayer?

Prayer is calling on God to show you great and mighty things that you don't know. This is talking to God. Ever since Adam told God that the woman you gave to me made me to sin, God said if that's the case, go and find your wife by yourself. He that finds a wife finds a good thing and obtains favour from the Lord. For the man he needs to pray to God to direct him to his wife and for the woman she needs to pray for a God-fearing man to locate her. Philippians 4:6.

Why must we pray?

Going to God in prayer is very necessary because that's the easiest way to surrender your problems, challenges to him, are you having a marriage burden in your heart? That is the time to go to God. Most singles don't go to God, they don't surrender to God in their waiting season instead they feel bitter and angry at God. This is not the time to be mad at God, it is the time to make your request known to Him because he is reliable, dependable and unchangeable, he is the one who sets the solitary in families, he is the one who has made promises and also the one who will make it come to pass when you call on him. Jeremiah 33:3. There are great and mighty things you don't know about your future spouse and marriage that God can show and reveal to you when you ask him to *Matthew 7:7 ask and it shall be given to you*. The bible says and you shall receive and that only he that asks must receive, if you have not asked for a colourful marriage then you are not ready to receive it. Our blessings are in God's hands but we need to ask for it before we can get it. The bible says we should work out our salvation with fear and trembling, so work it out in prayer.

HOW DO WE PRAY?

1. Pray in faith with the attitude to receive from God

2. Get a prayer journal and write down list of things you want God to do for you. God knows our desires even before we ask. You don't pray for your marriage when you are already married but before marriage,

list your marriage expectations to God.

3. Pray specifically Luke 18:34-40, specific prayer keeps your confidence high, increases your faith also, it helps you to know when God has answered it

WHAT ARE YOU PRAYING FOR?

For the spirit of wisdom

For discovery and pursuit and fulfillment of Gods purpose.

For your spouse to have a strong relationship with God likewise you.

For business prosperity

For God to bridle your tongues

For peace to reign in your home

Fruitfulness and children

Pray for your future spouse to be able to overcome temptation Pray for God's purpose over their lives to be fulfilled in a grand style

Pray for your spouse to have a stable relationship with God, pray that they are in line with God's will, pray for God to bless the works of his hands, pray that your spouse has community of believers, pray for protection over natural, physical and spiritual attacks, pray for your future spouse to have the mind of Christ, pray against any confusion. When they put God first, they will know how to love you the right way without compromising your relationship with God. Pray that he or she should be a person of integrity or honour. Pray that God should heal them from their past. Our past has a way of affecting our relationships because of the pains of the past are still on their minds you will start praying and battling with it, when it should have been tackled in prayer before you met. Pray for him to have divine wisdom, and that God should make you both whole in the waiting season. God delays seasons in our lives because he wants to work on us. Don't forget, you are also included in these prayers and after prayer you have to surrender it to God and see him doing it. ***Matthew 11:28 come*** *unto me all ye that have laboured and are heavy laden and I will give you rest.*

Pray, pray and pray. Don't get tired of praying.